THE
SOCIA[...]

Impact on t[...] world and the Birth of
Internationalism

ANDRE VLTCHEK

BADAK MERAH SEMESTA
2017

Andre Vltchek

The Great October Socialist Revolution

Copyright © 2017 by Andre Vltchek
All rights reserved

Cover Photos by: Andre Vltchek
Cover Design by: George Burchett
Layout by: Rossie Indira

First edition, 2017

Published by PT. Badak Merah Semesta
Jl. Madrasah Azziyadah 16, Jakarta
http://badak-merah.weebly.com
email: badak.merah.press@gmail.com

ISBN: 978-602-73543-9-5

ANDRE VLTCHEK

The Great October Socialist Revolution

By the same author

Exposing Lies of the Empire
Fighting Against Western Imperialism
On Western Terrorism: From Hiroshima to Drone Warfare (with Noam Chomsky)
The World Order and Revolution! (with Christopher Black & Peter Koenig)
Western Terror: From Potosi to Baghdad
Indonesia: Archipelago of Fear
Exile (with Pramoedya Ananta Toer & Rossie Indira)
Oceania – Neocolonialism, Nukes & Bones

Fiction:
Aurora
Point of No Return
Nalezeny
Plays: 'Ghosts of Valparaiso' and 'Conversations with James'

Content

Chapter 1 1
Chapter 2 9
Chapter 3 21
Chapter 4 29
Chapter 5 35
Chapter 6 45
Chapter 7 53
Chapter 8 69

About Author 75
Compliments 79

Andre Vltchek

1

*P*erhaps no other single event in modern history brought so much hope for humanity, as the Russian "Great October Socialist Revolution".

During those late autumn days of the year 1917, the entire world shook to its core. All previously accepted and incontestable foundations, on which the basic old perceptions of morality, justice, and also hope, faith and love were resting, began trembling, cracking and collapsing.

Tyrannical certitudes of obsolete and oppressive 'cultures', religions and regimes began collapsing like towers made of clay.

For some, these were completely intoxicating, and long expected moments of joy - true victory of reason and justice. A new dawn was here, and the New World had just been born. Slavery, servitude, humiliation and hopelessness were about to be swept away from the surface of the Earth, almost immediately and irreversibly.

For others, this was nothing less than the bitter end. Old certainties that used to govern over their existence, from religious faith to 'family values' and structures, were suddenly questioned openly and mercilessly; they were criticized, often labeled as absolute and smashed to pieces.

Those who used to govern and rule over millions were all of a sudden uncertain about the future. Tyrannical fathers and husbands became laughing stocks.

A new meaning was given to *The International*. It was not an abstract tune, anymore; everything was suddenly becoming real and reachable:

> *No more tradition's chains shall bind us*
> *Arise, ye slaves, no more in thrall;*
> *The earth shall rise on new foundations*
> *We have been naught we shall be all.*

It appeared that the entire world, in fact the entire universe, was suddenly ripe and ready for a spectacular and total reset. What seemed to be permanent and even sacred just at the onset of the previous night, looked suddenly shabby and completely outdated in the morning.

Everything changed: from how people walked, to how they smiled, how they addressed and greeted each other, how they perceived their elders or how they begged for pardons. Songs and rhythms also changed, and the way people danced. Colors and shapes altered and often, in such places that were once covered by an impenetrable darkness, a bright light now appeared suddenly and unexpectedly.

Russia, a deep but oppressed and fatalist giant, suddenly found itself at the epicenter of a grand explosion of colors and sounds, at the vanguard of the outstanding epic struggle against nihilism and backwardness. For centuries it went through hell and against hell it arose resolutely.

The greatest revolution in human history began.

*

On 25 October (7 November, New Style) 1917, the day the battleship "Aurora" fired its symbolic salvo at the Winter Palace in

Petrograd (now St. Petersburg), the entire world was awakened to an absolutely new reality.

"So, with the crash of artillery, in the dark, with hatred, and fear, and reckless daring, new Russia was being born." Wrote John Reed, an American author and journalist, who witnessed first-hand this amazing event that he then almost immediately celebrated in his immortal book "*Ten Days that Shook the World*".

John Reed came to a simple and powerful conclusion:

"Imagine this struggle being repeated in every barracks of the city, the district, the whole front, all Russia. Imagine the sleepless Krylenkos, watching the regiments, hurrying from place to place, arguing, threatening, entreating. And then imagine the same in all the locals of every labour union, in the factories, the villages, on the battle-ships of the far-flung Russian fleets; think of the hundreds of thousands of Russian men staring up at speakers all over the vast country, workmen, peasants, soldiers, sailors, trying so hard to understand and to choose, thinking so intensely-and

deciding so unanimously at the end. So was the Russian Revolution...."

Yes, for those who were oppressed, who struggled and suffered terribly, being shackled by the 'Old World' and its structures, the decision was almost unanimous indeed!

Suddenly, for individuals who clung to backward beliefs in 'holy Russia' or 'Tsarist fatherland', nothing appeared to be safe, anymore.

Fear spread with the speed of light, far beyond Russia's frontiers. Almost intuitively, Western imperialism and capitalism began to panic. They felt threatened, in fact vitally endangered. The revolutionaries were hungry, angry, outraged, and ready to openly defy and then challenge the greatest enemies of human kind: grotesque class divisions, embedded racism, atrocious imperialism and colonialism, as well as archaic family structures, religious 'beliefs' and power structures.

Along with false certitudes, fear also disappeared. All of a sudden, everything seemed to be possible, for Russia and for the entire world.

For the first time in human history, there was a great expectation that the world could improve and soon really belong fully to its people, and that the people would be able to form and re-form it, shape it so it could finally be there mainly in order to serve the long-suffering majority.

"Mankind - that has a proud sound!" wrote the great Soviet writer Maxim Gorky, one of the intellectual fathers of the Bolshevik Revolution.

After centuries and millennia of horror, plunder and misery... Yes, a proud and loud sound, finally!

Day one, year zero, and Russia was beginning to live again, after years and centuries of darkness, of hopelessness. An enormous nation was making its first steps, getting accustomed to an absolutely new reality, new circumstances!

It was not a simple process; nothing was easy at all. There was zeal and optimism, but also sorrow and immense struggle, and loss. There was inertia and several lapses.

But Russian people were used to all sorts of hardship. Throughout history they have struggled against countless (mostly Western) invasions, against extreme weather and other calamities. The war, WWI, was still raging, in the west, northwest and southwest. The new war, the civil war, soon engulfed almost the entire enormous territory of Russia, covering it with agony, and with an excruciating carpet of flames.

The oppressive forces of the previous regime waged continuous and vicious attacks against the new revolutionary state, its government and people. 'Elites', religious cadres, high-ranking military officers, stubborn landowners and businessmen, almost all of them were united, sparing no resources, doing all in their power to turn the clock of history decisively backwards. For some, particularly for those who used to be actively engaged in plundering 'old Russia' for centuries, it was nothing less than a bitter fight for survival. For the 'other side', for the revolutionaries and the awoken masses, the civil war became a monumental 'holy war', an epic struggle for a totally new and better country, as well as for universal justice and egalitarianism.

While the fury of civil war was raging, everything had to be re-thought and re-defined, from land issues and property rights to things like marriage (should marriage as an institutions survive in this new society?) and the rights of women. What kind of political, economic and social system should be implemented? Should the revolution first be won and solidified in one country, or should it be fought simultaneously all over the world? There were debates between Lenin and Trotsky, between those who trusted peasants and others who only trusted the workers.

Discussions were conducted everywhere; at workplaces and at dining tables in people's homes, even on street corners and on board long-distance trains as well as city trams. The debates were loud and passionate. People's voices were finally being heard and taken seriously. That itself was revolutionary, something unimaginable just hours before *"Aurora"* fired her first shot at the Winter Palace.

2

*H*undreds of thousands, perhaps even millions died. The civil war (1918-20) was brutal and devastating, while WWI was one of the deadliest in history. The two conflicts, at least for some time, raged simultaneously.

The revolutionaries wanted to end all wars immediately. Russian soldiers left their trenches, and embraced their enemies. "We are all brothers!" they shouted. "We were forced to fight each other by ruthless monarchs, priests and businessmen. We should battle real enemies, not each other! Proletariat of the world, Unite!" But the Western officers and commanders were determined: they forced their men back to the trenches, accusing them of treason, pushing them to the battlefields.

Most significantly, countless foreign invasions were overwhelming both several major Russian cities and the countryside. As always throughout the previous centuries, Europeans never thought twice before putting their military boots on Russian soil. In a way, Russia was treated and perceived as a 'barbaric' nation that could be attacked, colonized and plundered at will and without much justification, not unlike all those countless unfortunate nations all over the world: located in South America and Central Asia, in the Middle East, Africa, Asia and Oceania. Many Russians looked like whites, like Europeans, but to Westerners, they were never "white enough", never really part of the culture of the conquerors and plunderers. Russia always had its own soul, its way of thinking and feeling, its distinct manner of acting and reacting. In many ways (and not only geographically) it was and still is more Asian than European, and for that it has been despised in almost all Western capitals.

*

Internally, several military and political factions desperately opposed the Bolshevik Revolution. The "Russian Civil War" was fought by numerous groups, which included monarchists and militarists, with the great participation of foreign nationals. What is essential to understand is that virtually all opposition to the Bolshevik/Communist rule after the Great October Socialist Revolution, whether armed or political, was partially or even fully financed and sponsored from abroad.

Without grasping this fact, it is absolutely impossible to understand objectively what Western propaganda has been defining as the 'paranoia' of the Soviet leadership in the 1930's - its fixation on exposing the 'enemies of the state', uncovering of people spying for foreign powers, as well as those who had been involved in various acts of sabotage and the destabilization of the young Soviet socialist state.

What is being constantly omitted from almost all Western sources and historical accounts related to the Russian Civil War, is the shattering effect that foreign attacks, propaganda and the occupation of large territories had on the people of the new socialist and still largely defenseless nation. Much of the suffering and loss of human lives between the years of 1918 and 1921 can be traced to those 'interventions'.

The brutal, barbaric tactics that the West had been using so successfully against the post-1917 Russia were later (and with greater and smaller success) utilized against virtually all socialist and Communist countries, in all parts of the world.

The essence and strategy of Western imperialist subversion is essentially very simple: identify all strong and weak points of the country that you are attempting to murder, and try to comprehend its ideology. Study and learn all about its progressive leadership: its plans, and all that the revolution is trying to do for the people: like giving them frccdom, equal rights, improved life expectancy, high standards of education, medical care, housing, infrastructure, arts and overall decent quality of life. Then, attack where it hurts the most: use direct interventions, sabotage, terrorist assaults, or sponsor extremist and even religious fundamentalist groups, in order to spread fear and insecurity to slow down the process of social change and economic growth. Hit so hard that at some point, the democratic revolutionary system would have to react, simply in order to protect its people, their achievements, and even their bare lives. Wherever the West tries to destroy a socialist country, be it Nicaragua or Afghanistan in the 80's, it first targets hospitals and schools, in order to demolish the great social achievements of the government, and to spread hopelessness among the population. Then hit even harder, in order to trigger a strong government reaction, and then immediately declare: "You see, this is the real face of socialism or communism! You want a revolution? Fine: what you get in a package would be this: oppression, political trials, gulags, lack of freedom, and even some brutal executions!" Use widely, weapons like disinformation and negative propaganda, so the revolution in a progressive but cruelly terrorized country could never have a chance to really influence the rest of the world, and even at home it would begin to suffer after being under too much pressure: from serious ailments such as a lack of determination, confusion, cynicism as well as loss of faith. Take advantage of the fact that the world is still an extremely fragmented place, and people are actually in possession of very little knowledge about different parts of the planet (not much has changed in this respect in the last century, despite television, internet and other means of communication). At this point, when you have succeeded in spreading fear, nihilism, and while you have managed to put the government of the country you want to destroy on the defensive or even pushed into a corner, half of your battle is already won! You have managed to manufacture a real oppressor, a ruthless tyrant, and a 'brutal dictatorship'! Once you succeed, you can easily silence domestic opposition and begin direct support for the 'opposition' in those rebellious countries. If everything fails, you could, in many instances, invade yourself, benevolently 'liberating oppressed people' from 'tyranny'.

Such hideous tactics of the West, deeply injured the Soviet Union before WWII, but it failed to destroy the country.

In later years and decades, the techniques and battle tactics of Western imperialism were perfected, thoroughly and astoundingly. Dozens of countries collapsed under their attacks, from Iran, Iraq, Afghanistan, Egypt and Indonesia, to Chile and Nicaragua. Places like North Korea (DPRK), Cuba and Syria were forced to toughen up and radicalize their defenses, after countless embargos and even some deadly terrorist attacks.

*

Back to Russia: not long after the Revolution, foreign invaders began arriving from all corners of the Western world: France, Great Britain, the United States, Greece and Italy. There were also Czech, Romanian, Estonian, Polish and even Australian troops attacking the country, as did the mighty Japanese troops, which were responsible for countless atrocities in the eastern part of the country (recently I was told in the city of Vladivostok, how the Japanese Imperial Army used to burn Bolshevik commissars alive, inside railroad steam engines).

After the Revolution, all parts of the former Russian Empire were allowed to declare independence, if they so desired. Finland did so, and then, with German help, the Finnish aggressors pushed the Finnish-Russo border eastward, putting Petrograd almost within artillery range.

The British captured two important port cities in the north: Murmansk and Archangelsk, even setting up their client governments there.

The French were stationed in Ukraine.

Czech "Legions", at one point, managed to control the entire Trans-Siberian Railroad between the cities of Simbirsk (after 1924 known as Ulyanovsk) and Vladivostok, as well as an enormous territory north and south of the railway. They actively fought against the Bolsheviks, pillaging, raping and murdering in the areas that fell under their boots.

After declaring its independence in 1918, Poland decided to invade Ukraine in 1920. A brutal war followed. Eventually, the "Treaty of Riga" was signed on March 18th 1921, and about 10 million Ukrainians and Russians were placed under Polish rule.

One year later, in 1922, the Soviet Union (The Union of Soviet Socialist Republics, or USSR) was formed, which did not put an end to the foreign onslaughts.

Even the most unrealistically conservative Western estimates admit that at least 200,000 foreign troops fought against the Bolsheviks and the Revolution during the "Russian Civil War". Compared to the Red Army, they were extremely well armed and supplied, and capable of causing terrible damage.

*

Even before the years 1918-20, Russia had been continually invaded, primarily by Western powers. During such attacks, millions of people vanished and the country was fully destroyed. Having to fight so frequently for their bare survival, Russian people have been intuitively understanding of the sentiments of individuals of countless nations on all continents of the world that have been suffering under the brutal yoke of colonialism and imperialism.

Imperialist attacks against their socialist motherland and Revolution, hardened the Russian nation even further, bringing a new level of determination and consciousness to its people. The conclusion of the original, and in that period still evolving ideology, was obvious and logical: "In the name of world peace, in the name of global justice, and especially in the name of survival of mankind, imperialism has to be fought decisively, and defeated in all parts of the world. There should be no colonialist practices left anywhere on our Planet, colonialism has to be defeated and destroyed, once and for all".

Here, on the battlefields of the Russian Civil War, modern Internationalism was born!

Almost immediately, the Western imperialist regimes understood the importance of the event, as well as its implications. The decision was made rapidly: "This system - this new revolutionary Internationalism and its ideology, theories and practice - are the most dangerous antagonists of the Western geopolitical and commercial interests. They are directly challenging the Western dominance over the Planet. They would soon influence and inspire dozens of oppressed and usurped nations all over the world; they'd give them hope, as well as ideology and strength to fight their cruel imperialist tormentors. Therefore, the Soviet Communists and Internationalists have to be fought, destroyed, in fact annihilated, and their thoughts should be fully erased from the consciousness of all people, as promptly as possible. Even after being defeated and destroyed, their ideals have to be smeared, ridiculed and discredited, posthumously, by all means, and in all corners of the world."

It was clear to the rulers in London, Paris, Berlin and Washington that the Soviet Union was able to inspire the entire oppressed world and to lead it to independence and freedom.

The West in general and its ideologues in particular, got at that point clearly and impressively 'farsighted'. In their imagination and with their predictions, they were even one step ahead of Russia itself (and of the Soviet Union shortly after). They identified and forecast many fierce battles that would soon begin shaping the future of our Planet - the battles that would be fought for true and sacred freedom, for independence, and against imperialist tyranny. They predicted all this, and actually they did it even several years before the first modern-day anti-colonialist fights could truly begin (and in which the USSR would full-heartedly get involved in).

This is how the irreconcilable conflict between the nihilism of imperialism/colonialism and optimism of Internationalism came to life; how the struggle, which is raging to this very day, suddenly erupted.

3

*F*or centuries, Russia was a feudal country. Only by a decree issued by Tsar Alexander II in 1861, was serfdom abolished. That was only 56 years before the start of the Great October Socialist Revolution. But even right before the Bolsheviks took power in two major cities of the empire (Petrograd and Moscow) in 1917, conditions in most of the Russian countryside and even in some provincial towns continued to be thoroughly appalling. Wealth disparities were great, while the voices of common people could hardly be heard. The situation was not as bad as in the colonies occupied and plundered by the UK, France, Netherlands, Belgium or Germany, but it was very cruel nevertheless.

Significantly, serfdom in Russia was not

race-related; it was a complex and unsettling phenomenon, which victimized millions of both white and blue-eyed Orthodox Christian men, women and children, as well as millions of 'others' (people belonging to various ethnic and religious groups) that inhabited the vast territories of the Russian Empire, from Europe to Central Asia and all the way to the Far East.

By the time "Aurora" fired its first salvo at the symbol of imperial oppression – the Winter Palace – most of the long-suffering Russian people were ready for a prolonged struggle for an egalitarian society. The brutality of the oppression of the masses before the Great October Socialist Revolution gave birth to several rebellions, to the 1905 revolution, then to almost permanent popular outrage. The deeply-rooted desire to create a new system based on the principles of permanent social justice, first for Russia, and eventually for the rest of the world, was engulfing entire vast country.

At the beginning of the 20th Century, there were numerous fundamental differences between life in Russia and life in Western Europe.

In the West, the rulers allowed their citizens at least a certain degree of freedom, providing at least some social stability. The standard of living in the UK, France, the United States and elsewhere in the industrialized West had been consistently growing for decades, at least before the start of WWI. However, the question that would be asked very soon, would cut through the core: "who was actually paying the bill for such 'altruism'?"

Of course, true horrors were not taking place anywhere inside the boundaries of the West (if one doesn't count the horrors and slaughter of tens of millions of innocent civilians and soldiers during the WWI), they were occurring somewhere 'far away', in the "rest of the world", where both Europe and increasingly the United Sates were mercilessly massacring and plundering entire conquered continents, while filling their own coffers, beautifying their cities and enjoying high arts and culture.

European colonialists 'opened the veins' of Central and South America. They stole everything they could lay their hands on: in what is now Peru, Bolivia, Ecuador, Brazil, Chile and Mexico, as well as in so many other places in so-called Latin America. They did it first directly, through atrocious invasions, and later through 'trade', using morally and financially corrupt local elites, many of them of European stock.

They murdered millions or even tens of millions, showing no mercy and absolutely no humanity. People in the colonies were regularly treated like animals; the entire concept of 'human rights' was exclusively applicable to white Europeans and North Americans. In some places, particularly on certain islands, Westerners managed to exterminate almost everybody, demonstrating much greater ruthlessness than even the US neo-colonialists who have often murdered "only a fraction" of its victims in occupied territories. In some instances, the French butchered 100% or almost 100% of the native local population, as happened for instance during their reign of Grenada, or in the Polynesian Easter Islands where over 90% vanished.

Europe has been committing slaughters, on unimaginable scales, in almost all corners of the globe. For instance, the

Belgian king Leopold II was responsible for the loss of around 10 million human lives in Congo, in the days when what is now known as the Congo (DRC and Congo-Brazzaville) had just a fraction of the population that it now possesses. Entire families, millions of them, living in the countryside, were locked in their huts and burned alive, while millions of others had their hands amputated, literally chopped off, for 'being lazy' and not working fast enough on the rubber plantations.

When it comes to the list of crimes against humanity committed by Europe, in the past and present, I never know where to begin and where to end. The list is simply so long and too horrible. An entire sizeable book would, perhaps, be needed to compile at least some extremely basic catalogue.

Such a list would have to include the German holocaust against the local people of what is now Namibia; the Belgian super-genocides in all of their 'dependencies', the Dutch plunder of what is now Indonesia, brutal French rule in Indochina, the Portuguese inefficient but deadly plunder of Brazil. It would have to describe bestialities that Western invaders committed in India and China, Italian barbarities in Africa, and of course both the British and French holocausts there, the slave trade, pillage and plunder in basically all the continents of the world, something that actually continues to this very day, to a great extent unopposed and generally ignored.

Not long before the Great October Socialist Revolution began liberating oppressed people all over the Russian Empire, the United States managed to murder around one million people in the Philippines, which was then its crown colony. Some victims were combatants – true patriots and freedom fighters - but most of them were just defenseless civilians.

Despite the great fragmentation of the world, Russian revolutionary intellectuals were well aware of the state in which most of the Planet had to fight for its survival. In Petrograd and Moscow, there was a natural sympathy and solidarity towards the oppressed people of the world. Although the initial attempts of the Russian revolutionaries were to radicalize Europe, seeking alliances in Germany, France, Hungary, Spain and elsewhere, the focus eventually shifted towards Asia, Africa and other parts of the planet that were enslaved and humiliated by Western imperialism and colonialism.

At the start, the Bolsheviks had hoped for a series of revolutions to rock Europe and to overthrow imperialist regimes. That would have created new alliances and stopped all anti-Russian aggressions from the west. But European revolutions, from Hungary to Germany had failed. It indicated even then, that European workers and the middle class were already at least partially bought and corrupted by the system, and therefore unwilling to sacrifice the dividends from the enormous booty (at least to some extent shared among all citizens of the colonialist and imperialist powers) that was ceaselessly flowing from the devastated and humiliated colonies.

Although life in the Russian countryside before the Revolution was not as extreme as in most of the colonies controlled by Western imperialist powers, the Russian people were able to understand and identify with the suffering of Africans and

Asians. Intuitively, they decided to spread their own struggle to the rest of the world. From the outset, there were some basic disagreements between major Soviet leaders: while Lenin and Stalin were basically advocating first building a strong socialist state in one country, Trotsky believed in global revolution, in parallel revolutionary struggles in several parts of the world. However, scholars and theoreticians often exaggerate these differences: both Lenin and Stalin were actually also strong believers in a global struggle and Internationalism, and their attempt to first solidify revolutionary achievements in Russia (and consequently in the Soviet Union) was nothing other than a strategic maneuver.

The deafening salvo from the battleship Aurora, and the heroic charge against the Winter Palace, was in fact the great beginning of the first truly Internationalist struggle; one that would later be understood, modified and carried on in several other centers of heroic resistance against Western imperialism, such as Havana, Beijing, Hanoi, Caracas and Damascus.

4

As Western anti-Soviet and anti-Communist propaganda shifted into top gear, all that is stated above got completely ignored. The *leitmotif* became predictable and primitive: 'excesses and crimes' committed under the Bolsheviks during and after the 1917 Revolution, as well as under Stalin's government, which lasted from his ascent to power in the 1920's, till his death in 1953. Nothing is usually mentioned about what triggered the 'reaction'. As if the 'action' never took place and the reaction appeared unexpectedly, without any substantial reason. Erased were almost all references to Western invasions of the country, all subversions and other acts of terror unleashed against the young revolutionary state. As if the enemies of the Soviet Union were all imaginary, as if all fears of the Soviet leaders for the survival of their country (and the world) were only the results of their dictatorial tendencies and psychological disorders!

This propaganda, repeated thousands of times all over Europe, North America and inside their 'client' states, eventually fully domesticated, in fact converted itself into the mainstream narrative and interpretation of history.

Anyone with even a drop of objectivity would have to admit (unless he or she was fully set on denying the basic principle of humanism, which declares that all people are equal, regardless of their race and or nationality) that the Communist Soviet Union committed a much lower amount of crimes than Western countries under the banner of 'constitutional monarchies' or 'multi-party democracies'.

While the Soviets were busy pulling tens of millions of people out of poverty (and we are talking, for instance, about the Muslims of the Soviet Middle East, the areas where the standard of living eventually reached that of the European parts of Russia, as well as the other countless minorities inhabiting this enormous country), in approximately the same period of history the Europeans managed to kill, as was mentioned above, around 10 million people in Central and West Africa alone, chopping off their hands and burning women and children in their huts alive.

The British Empire was running several concentration camps all over the African continent simultaneously; it was bombing and gassing civilians in the Middle East ("We reserve our right to bomb those niggers", to borrow from the colorful vocabulary of the British Prime Minister Lloyd George), and it triggered several brutal famines all over the Sub-Continent (including Churchill's brainchild - the great famine of Bengal), which took the lives of dozens of millions of human beings.

The genocides, mass murder and terror spread by the West, in the rest of the world, are countless, but of course under-reported, as 'foreign aid' for education and the media, has managed to train and discipline collaborators in the poor parts of the world, securing that the truth about the past would be generally omitted or downplayed even in those countries that have been brutalized by the West incessantly (this trend is now clearly evident for instance in Afghanistan, Kenya, India and Indonesia, and before Duterte's administration came to power, it was reaching absolutely grotesque proportions in the Philippines).

Even the end of WWII did not bring an end to the savage treatment of 'the natives' at the hands of the European and North American colonialists. One should recall the treatment of the people of the Middle East, by Winston Churchill and other glorified British leaders. All this is of course is well documented, including in books written by Churchill himself, but hardly mentioned by the disciplined and reliable mainstream media and academia, in both the colonizing and colonized nations.

There are countless statues of Winston Churchill and the Belgian King, Leopold II, all over the capitals of Europe.

*

The Soviet Union confronted the entire Western imperialist and colonialist system directly, full force. It did it altruistically, in the great spirit of humanism and solidarity. Its people sacrificed millions of their lives and many creature comforts. Their fight was noble - to liberate the entire enslaved world. It is therefore not surprising that London, Paris, New York and other Western capitals mobilized tremendous resources, in order to destroy both the great socialist country and its ideology, dragging them through dirt, inventing or at least greatly exaggerating their 'crimes', belittling the achievements.

For Western imperialists and pillagers, it has been one colossal fight for survival. To destroy the Soviets, to smear their ideals, tens of millions were butchered, 'sacrificed', annihilated: from dozens of Latin American countries longing for socialism, to dozens of nations in Africa, but also Iran, Vietnam, Laos, Cambodia, Indonesia, to name just a few. Lies have been piling on top of lies; entire generations of people have been indoctrinated through education, culture and direct propaganda.

In the West and in its colonies, almost no one knows anything about Soviet or even world history, but people are parroting several slogans to oblivion, as if in some Orwellian or Kafkaesque nightmare: "Stalinism", "gulags", and "violations of human rights".

Very few understand the essence and depth of both the Great October Socialist Revolution and Soviet Union: It was all not only about the economic and social system. Above all, to be a Soviet Communist has meant to be a fighter in an epic and perpetual struggle against Western imperialism!

5

*I*n Russia and the Soviet Union, for strategic and humanitarian reasons, the first half of the 20th Century was mainly dedicated to solidifying Communist rule, as well as to industrialization, education and the construction of a solid scientific platform in this once deprived and backward part of the world. In that period of history, and mainly due to the great hope and enthusiasm triggered by both the Great October Socialist Revolution and the evolution of the socialist state, the Soviet Union achieved the fastest economic growth of any country on Earth, in any historical period. Almost total access to electricity was accomplished, new roads and railroads constructed, tens of thousands of schools and hospitals built. The Soviet Union reached almost a 100%

literacy rate. Its newly-educated people were suddenly able to design as well as produce anything from giant turbines, to some of the most advanced airplanes on Earth.

This was the specter, the most horrid monster and nightmare for Western demagogues and reactionaries: a socialist or a Communist country capable of standing firmly on its feet, of building bridges, skyscrapers, giant ships and locomotives, a nation, which inspired some of the greatest musicians, poets, writers and dancers, and where great arts suddenly belonged to everyone. This was a place where even a cleaning lady or a janitor could afford to visit an opera house performance, and eat open sandwiches with black caviar during the intermission, downing it with a glass of decent local sparkling wine.

For the West and its classist, racist and elitist system, this was something thoroughly unacceptable. Such a system was seen as sick, deranged, extremely dangerous, and it had to be destroyed by all means! Otherwise the rot could easily spread all over the world. Otherwise it could contaminate even the very centers of world finance, or imperialism and colonialism.

For decades, the Western regime studied and analyzed all possible scenarios that could help it to achieve its main goal: to damage and finally destroy the land of the Soviets, to stop the clock of history and to reverse progress.

Instead of zealous optimism, the brotherhood of men, an egalitarian society, instead of the joy of giving, of creating a new country and a truly new world, the Western regime was dreaming about preserving slavery in most parts of the world, it was fighting to uphold elitism based strictly on lineage and the white race, on private property and profits, and on outdated religious dogmas and demagogy.

The showdown was inevitably approaching; the battle between the legacies of the October Revolution, versus the powerful reactionary forces united under such banners as 'conservative and religious values', 'civilization' and 'Western culture'.

*

Then came WWII, and the epic struggle of the Soviet people against Nazism and fascism. At least 25 million Soviet people lost their lives, fighting one of the most dreadful monsters in human history. Most definitely, the monster was 'one of the most dreadful', but not '*the* most dreadful'; because right from the start, both fascism and Nazism were constructed on the principles of Western imperialism, racism and colonialism. What the West was doing to all parts of the world, for long and awful centuries, it suddenly dared to unleash against the people living on its territory: Jews and Roma, Slavs and the disabled.

In most parts of Europe, fascist and Nazi sentiments resonated often very positively. Entire countries became fascist or Nazi overnight, from Spain and Portugal to Hungary, Slovakia, Romania, Bulgaria, Italy and of course Germany itself. In both the UK and France, Nazism enjoyed a great following.

The United States was first extremely reluctant to join the struggle against Nazism and fascism. Both were often intertwined ideologically: Henry Ford inspired Adolf Hitler, and vice versa. The US concept of 'advertisement' had a great influence on Nazi propaganda techniques (and one could say again, "and vice versa"). It is now hardly addressed by the mainstream press and educational facilities, but right before WWII, the United States was still one of the most racially segregated places on Earth. Technically, 'the land of the free'; was an apartheid state!

There was only one country on Earth, in that period of history, which could stand up, proudly, throw itself on the battlefield, and in tremendous but beautiful sacrifice, defeat the sickening plague of Nazi hordes. It was, of course, the Soviet Union!

The reason was simple: the Soviet Union and its people were fighting for the survival of the entire humankind, not just for their own devastated Motherland, and definitely not for some geopolitical interests.

Soviet soldiers marched to Berlin, and on the other side of the world, they fought alongside their Chinese brothers, the great People's Liberation Army, helping China to defeat another malicious and close ally of Western imperialists – Japan.

Only true Internationalist spirit was capable of saving our planet from colossal peril.

And it did. At an immense price, but it did!

Instead of gratitude (by now it is clear that the Western imperialist culture and propaganda machine are hardly capable of such emotions as gratitude), the great Soviet sacrifice was belittled, and then even dragged through dirt. Instead of comparing two almost similar coins - Western colonialism/imperialism and racism with German and Italian Nazism and fascism – the official mouthpieces of the West got busy trying to debauch history by comparing Nazism with 'Stalinism', essentially spitting on the graves of the 25 million Soviet people who nobly and altruistically saved the world from imminent ruin, with the name of their leader, Joseph Stalin, on the lips.

That's how imperialism functions and survives: by spreading dogmas, lies and negativism, and by utilizing its perfectly functioning indoctrination apparatus, which has been regurgitating and disseminating until now, the most effective propaganda on Earth.

*

In the second half of the 20th Century, during the so-called 'Cold War', the Soviet Union stood firmly on the side of the oppressed, on the side of liberation struggles, and for freedom in Africa, Asia and Latin America. One has to wonder how mighty the disinformation campaign has had to be to have made all this 'forgotten'?

While Europe and the United States (and their constitutional monarchies and multi-party 'democracies') cultivated despots in Iran, Egypt, the Gulf, the Middle East, South Vietnam, Cambodia, South Korea, Chile, Argentina, Guatemala, Nicaragua, Uruguay, the Dominican Republic, Haiti, Brazil, Kenya, South Africa, Indonesia and so many other unfortunate places, the Soviet Union stood by the Cuban, Nicaraguan, Tanzanian and North Vietnamese revolutions, it supported the leaders, true heroes and liberators, such as Patrice Lumumba of Congo and President Salvador Allende of Chile.

Both of us – Noam Chomsky and I –

came to the conclusion during our recent debate at the MIT, that the standards of living in Riga, Prague or East Berlin were "allowed to be" significantly higher than in Moscow, while those of Tashkent or Samarkand were just marginally lower. The standard of living in the colonies and the 'client' states of the West were ten, twenty, even a hundred times lower than those in Washington, Paris or London, often resulting in the loss of millions of human lives due to misery, even famines.

I calculated that some 55 million lives have been lost since WW II, as a result of Western colonialism, neocolonialism, direct invasions, sponsored coups and other acts of international terror. I am probably grossly under-estimating the numbers, as there have been lives lost due to hunger and malnutrition, treatable diseases, terrible mismanagement, and the outright misery triggered by Western imperialism and neo-colonialism.

Tens of millions of lives were further lost as a result of planting the terrible seeds of the 'divide and rule' strategy, the most obvious and horrid case being the "Partition" of the Sub-Continent.

Inspired by the principles and ideals of the Great October Socialist Revolution, the Soviet Union was on many historical occasions the only beacon of hope for oppressed people in all corners of the world.

It was not only the armed struggle against colonialism that Moscow was supporting. There were entire dedicated publishing houses in the former USSR, which were printing millions of books in all languages of the world, including the tiniest ones, almost extinct, in Asia, Africa and elsewhere. These books were then distributed, for free or for a symbolic price, to all parts of the world, wherever they were needed, wherever local culture appeared to be in danger.

That's the spirit of Internationalism!

Tens of thousands of students from poor countries, including Africa, Latin America and Asia, annually descended on Moscow, Kiev, Leningrad, Kharkov and other major Soviet cities, in order to receive free high-quality education.

Soviet cultural centers in India, Egypt, Afghanistan and countless other countries, were overflowing with classical music records (LP's), books and educational materials.

The West, and its mass media and propaganda outlets, liked to call all this a 'rivalry', between what they called cynically, the 'free world', and the socialist bloc countries.

But in reality, often clumsily and not always effectively, the Soviet Union, until the end of its existence inspired by the ideals of the Great October Socialist Revolution, was doing exactly what its early-day revolutionaries had promised to the masses: it was educating people regardless of their race or position, it was trying to cure the ill, it was bringing culture and arts to the cities as well as the countryside, and it was fighting against all sorts of racial discrimination.

6

The West never 'forgave' those countries that stood in way of absolute global supremacy.

Those nations that dared to resist, were smashed to pieces: from Afghanistan to Indonesia, from Yugoslavia to Chile.

The Union of the Soviet Socialist Republics, a colossus that was built on the legacy of the Great October Socialist Revolution, became the first determinedly anti-colonialist and anti-imperialist power in the history of mankind. For that reason alone, it simply had to be destroyed. Its annihilation became the mainstay of Western foreign policy, for years and for decades.

In 1979, the West tricked the Soviet Union and its Red Army into entering its fraternal neighbor - Afghanistan.

Immediately after that, it mobilized the vilest extremist religious forces on Earth, paid them through its allies in the Gulf as well as Pakistan, armed them, later, and eventually both Afghanistan and the Soviet Union were mercilessly destroyed.

Now I work intensively in Afghanistan, driving all around the country, visiting villages and cities, talking to people. I'm writing a book about this amazing but scarred place. Despite what the world has been told by the mainstream propaganda apparatus, Afghans still love Russians. They consider them their brothers, and they remember with tears in their eyes, their kindness and their warmth.

*

The Soviet Union fell, "collapsed" in the most absurd way, in unimaginable pain and agony.

It was financially exhausted from the well-calculated arms race initiated by both the US and Western European. Nihilism and cynicism poisoned it. They were injected through Western propaganda media outlets, directed at all cities in the

Soviet Union and its allies. The war in Afghanistan was the final blow.

The inept and pathetic 'leadership' of Mikhail Gorbachev was followed by the treasonous alcoholic stupor reign of the West's favorite - Boris Yeltsin, who literally broke his huge and powerful country into pieces.

The Russians were fooled, humiliated, and for the first time in centuries, forced onto their knees. But no help arrived. The social state decomposed, the medical system collapsed, education was westernized and it collapsed as well, while life expectancy dropped to sub-Saharan African levels. The Yeltsin era was marked by shooting and murdering pro-Soviet protesters, by leading scientists from Novosibirsk and elsewhere selling their books in the bitter cold in metro underpasses, by old people freezing to death because their pensions were cancelled, by unpaid salaries, by a collapsing currency, war in Chechnya, the introduction of savage capitalism and horrifying crime rates.

The West cheered. It danced. It refused to honor the treaties it signed with

Gorbachev, its companies began stripping the entire country of its assets, and the most talented Soviet people were siphoned abroad.

Everything came to complete standstill. It was not as horrible as the Chinese era of humiliation by the West, but it was horrible enough.

Then, slowly but majestically, Russia rose from its knees.

Still, it cannot be called Communist as before, but it is definitely far from being capitalist in a Western sense. Most importantly, it has managed to recover economically, and to reintroduce a sound social system.

Its foreign policy is based on similar internationalist principles as those of former the Soviet Union. Russia is once again the best friend of oppressed people worldwide, and the mortal enemy of Western imperialism.

The West hates it as much as it used to hate the Soviet Union, which could be taken as a clear proof that Moscow is on the right track.

*

There may be no country called the Soviet Union anymore, but even its legacy gives shivers of fear and nightmares to the captains of the Western-imposed global regime, whether they are seated in Washington, London, or anywhere else.

The legacies of both the Great October Socialist Revolution and the Soviet Union are still being unfailingly smeared, in all mainstream Western media outlets, from the right to the 'soft anti-Communist left'. Historical facts, even the languages are being twisted and manipulated. Negative, depressing falsehoods have been inserted into the official narrative. Fabrications are passed as facts, even as educational materials.

The greatest adversary to Western imperialism and colonialism so far, the Soviet country, its Revolution, its ideology and even its great leaders, are slowly being transformed into monsters, presented as coldblooded murderers. In the West, this perverse manipulation of the truth is turning into a bizarre art form, into an obsession, hysteria, and into something that could only be compared to religious fundamentalism.

In March 2017, The Royal Academy of Arts in London launched a huge exhibition; "Revolution – Russian Art 1917-1932". The works of some of the greatest Soviet artists of all forms and genres, from Eisenstein to Malevich, Shostakovich to Gorky, were represented there. Film clips were shown, music played, paintings were put on the walls. But this greatest art of the 20th Century had to share space with some of the most professional and vicious outbursts of British propaganda! Almost all events, all artists, were smeared, ridiculed or turned into 'opposition figures'. Visitors were clearly instructed what to think, how to react. Revolutionary art was stripped off its optimism, enthusiasm. Western propaganda was clearly acting as an antidote to revolutionary zeal. Instead of being inspired, happy and rebellious, I felt defeated, leaving the exhibition feeling sick, depressed and angry.

*

In the meantime, Russia is becoming more and more Soviet, again. It is not alone.

This time it is not relying on false allies in the former East European bloc. It embraces real comrades in China, Latin America and other progressive parts of the planet.

The entire world is watching. The West is shaking in fear and so are those who are collaborating with the Western regime.

The Great October Socialist Revolution is not dead, far from it! Its ideals went through agonizing tests, but they passed with flying colors.

"It is time to undust old banners", the legendary South American revolutionary writer, Eduardo Galeano, once told me, not long before he passed away.

Now the banners are flying again and they are flying high.

7

How did the Great October Socialist Revolution influence the people? I went to my comrades and colleagues in several parts of the world, asking this exact question.

"Bolsheviks and proletarian internationalism" is a brief study written by Artem Kirpichenok, a prominent Russian Marxist historian, a graduate of Jerusalem University (Ph.D.) exclusively for this slim book. Mr. Kirpichenok now resides in St-Petersburg, Russia again, where he works as a historian, journalist and a blogger:

"From the beginning, proletarian internationalism was a very important part of the Bolshevik movement, for three different and significant reasons: First, Bolshevism was born as part of the

international social-democratic movement and never saw itself removed from the global workers' movement. Before WWI, leaders like Lenin and Trotsky, as well as other Russian Bolsheviks, took part in the international labor mobilization during the social-democratic congresses. Second: the Bolshevik party itself always included people from different nations of the Russian Empire and some parts of Europe – Lenin was Russian, but Stalin was Georgian, Trotsky was a Jew, Enessa Armand (one of Lenin's close friends and aides was French) etc. The last point I'd like to make – proletarian internationalism was an important element for the Bolsheviks, because of the international nature of the working class itself, in that historic period, like today, when mass migration brings to all industrial centers people of many different nationalities. In St Petersburg about half of the professional workers were Latvians, Finns, Germans and Estonians. In Baku, which used to be the center of Russian oil industry, most workers were Azeri, Russians, Armenians,

Iranians as well as Georgians. In Donbas industrial areas, most workers were Russians, Ukrainians and Poles. And in such a reality of the proletarian togetherness, the internationalism was not just some beautiful rhetoric, but the only way for the workers' movement to succeed.

On November 1917 the Bolsheviks triggered the Revolution. But the situation in Russia remained extremely difficult for them. The Russian army almost collapsed, under the German offensive. The frontline kept moving eastward. Both industry and transportation were paralyzed, while agriculture remained desperately undeveloped. New revolutionary states could count on almost no friend and allies from abroad. In those days (as well as now) the ruling classes around the globe hated the Bolsheviks even more then they'd now hate an Islamic state. Lenin understood that the only friend and staunch ally of Russia was the global working class. Only solidarity of workers could bring real peace to Russia, to modernize the country.

Lenin was not a utopian; he saw the situation in the world very clearly, and his work was tactically brilliant. In November 1918, the German Revolution erupted. When the German workers and sailors crashed the Kaiser's regime, Soviet Russia managed to free itself from the "Brest Peace Treaty" and eventually achieved liberation from German occupation. A few years later, massive workers protests literally paralyzed both British and French intervention against Soviet Russia. That was a good beginning, but Lenin had much bigger plans. He believed in a global Revolution, or at least in an emergence of the Socialist States of Europe. For him, such a development was the most certain way to modernize Russia. How? After the capitalist states and empires would collapse, Russia would receive German and other technologies from European workers, while sending back to Central and Western Europe things it had in abundance, including food and natural resources. It all looked very promising. Between 1918 and 1921 revolutions or rebellions erupted on the territory of almost every European country. The most significant revolutions took place in Germany (Bavaria) and Hungary. There was a military rebellion in Holland, as well as the so-called 'Red Year' in Italy. General strikes and uprisings were taking Spain and Italy by storm, while Irish people commenced their war of independence, against the British Empire. However, the social democrats began betraying the European revolutions, and at the end, Lenin's hopes for the Socialist States of Europe were never fulfilled. The modernization of Soviet Russia finally took place, in the early 1930's, but the process became much more dramatic and painful than was originally expected. In the end, it didn't come because of positive involvement from the friendly socialist countries, but because of the internal mobilization of resources.

At the end, Lenin confronted leading imperialist countries, and launched a totally new strategy. He clearly realized that in 1918-1921, several important socialist and anti-colonial rebellions were taking place in the countries of Africa, Asia and Latin America. In 1920 the

Bolsheviks organized the congress of Asian and other colonized nations in Baku. During the congress, the new tactics and strategies of close cooperation with all oppressed nations around the globe were announced. Capitalists and imperialists put to use resources from the plundered countries for corrupting 'worker's aristocracy' in Europe and in North America. They also used the colonies as secure markets for their goods. The plan of the Bolsheviks was to help trigger several anti-colonialist and anti-imperialist global revolutions, and to destabilize the entire Western expansionist system. These tactics were then used by the Bolsheviks for decades."

Moscow continues to support various anti-imperialist struggles all over the world, while it stands firmly by several countries that are resisting Western neo-colonialist occupation and plunder. The best example is Syria, where the onslaught of Western imperialism and its most reliable ally – Islamic fundamentalism – has been decisively stopped, at a terrible price but stopped nevertheless.

*

Néstor Gorojovsky, an Argentinian thinker, is one of the most respected intellectuals in his country. He replied to me from Buenos Aires, paying tribute to the greatness of the October Revolution, while also warning that, like in China, the Latin American Revolutions should have their own personality, reflecting their national character:

"The Russian Revolution of 1917 was like a solar flare that, in some way or other, illuminated the entire planet Earth. However, this immense burst of light reached different places in different ways.

In Latin America, the Russian Revolution, of course, aroused every socialist dream among the exploited people who took notice of the enormous historic event. It also has had a strong influence in shaping the ideas of the Latin American radical minded youth ever since.

However, many of those young people

who have been influenced by the Russian Revolution, erroneously and (what a paradox of history!) in a colonial bend of mind, believe that in order to solve Latin American problems it would be enough to just copy the "lessons of Red October". Actually, this is a great mistake. Devising the way in order to carry on our own revolution is, of course, our own task. In fact, what we must do is to be faithful to the message of the Great Russian revolution and others that followed, but also to be ourselves, not to copy anything, and arise.

If October 1917 had not challenged Western European punditry, and Russians had not started a proletarian revolution in a predominately peasant country, our world would now be very different, and almost certainly extremely 'gloomy'. That is the greatest lesson we can learn from October 1917, here in Latin America.

As an eventful and long century flowed through the gates of history, we Latin Americans have learnt many other lessons as to how our own battles must be waged. Many of them came from the Red

October, but others are deeply rooted in our own peculiarities.

Today, the October Revolution is still like the brightest imaginable beacon that helps us to map the road towards a humane world of equality and liberty for the entire world and mankind. It has explained to us, sometimes through Moor's splendid propaganda imagery, sometimes through the acts and writings of its great leaders, that we shall never be truly free until the snake of imperialism is finally beheaded.

Just like the Chinese Revolution of 1949, the Great October Socialist Revolution taught us that we, Latin Americans, must be always faithful to ourselves, build our struggle on the socialist foundations of the great and united Latin American Nation for which our Liberators fought with such passion, and that only the complete uprooting of capitalism could open the gates and give birth to a new humankind, in fact the first real humankind that would have ever stepped on the vast spaces of our planet Earth."

Arthur Tewungwa, an important Ugandan opposition politician, an aide to the President Of The Uganda People's Congress (UPC) expressed his views from Kampala:

"Academically, post-colonial Africa has always been overly influenced by the Western imperialist nations, as a legacy of that unfortunate epoch. This led to limited understanding, let alone knowledge of the 1917 Great October Socialist Revolution. However, those individuals who were leaning towards the left of the political sphere led our great independence struggles. This has resulted in a sentiment that lends to the notion that the Revolution was the catalyst to the liberation struggle on the continent that was underway albeit, in a limited way, and provided the ideological drive missing in that struggle."

*

Ms. Zeinab Al-Saffar, an Iraqi educator, journalist and researcher connected the legacy of the October Revolution with the on-going plight of the Palestinian people:

"The centennial to the Great October Social Revolution this year coincides with 100 years since the ominous Balfour Declaration was produced, which led to the confiscation of the land from its real owners, the Palestinian people.

What the Palestinians are in dire need of are the underlying humanitarian principals of the Red October uprising, but with the emphasis on maintaining respect for all religions and faiths, for all people and their particularities. We all need those powerful slogans like 'end the war!' as much as we need all the Palestinians to return to their land based on another potent motto: 'All Land To All!', be it Muslims or non-Muslims, rich or poor, peasants or masters.

Just as the October Revolution was the culmination of a long period of repression and unrest, the Palestinians need a multi-colored worldwide revolution that will bring to a halt the offensive oppression by the ongoing Israeli onslaught, settlements and occupation."

*

A legendary Filipino academic, Prof. Roland Simbulan, who teaches at the Department of Social Sciences of the University of the Philippines (UP),

"The 1917 socialist revolution in Russia for the first time transformed socialist theory and practice into a material force and reality. From now on, here was a socialist country and model that challenged capitalist development and the U.S. expansion worldwide. The global balance of power became more favorable for the growth and strengthening of the working class and liberation movements, particularly in Asia and the Philippines. For soon after socialist led liberation movements were established in Asia including the Philippines, where an advanced detachment of the labor movement organized in 1930 the Communist Party of the Philippines led by Crisanto Evangelista.

Soon after the 1917 Great October Socialist Revolution, Russia immediately fostered international solidarity. It became a sanctuary and point of

convergence between and among fraternal proletarian parties in capitalist countries and national liberation movements from the colonies."

Dr. Taher Moktar, 'a socialist Egyptian physician', is a revolutionary and a former prisoner of conscience. He wrote to me from Europe, explaining how the Great October Revolution influenced him personally:

"100 years have passed since the Great October Socialist Revolution, which took place in Russia in 1917. 100 years since the beginning of one of the most inspirational events in human history. Whatever the results are, this revolution will remain one of the extremely important marks in the struggle of mankind towards freedom and rights.

The Great October Socialist Revolution had a huge effect on me personally, on both political and revolutionary levels. Before the Egyptian revolution in 2011, I had very little knowledge about revolutions in history, and when the Egyptian revolution started, I was wondering about other revolutions in history: how the revolutionaries behaved, and how they dealt with the counterrevolutions. Of all revolutions in history, two revolutions that grasped my attention the most were the French and the October revolutions. I actually became a revolutionary socialist through reading about the October Revolution. And almost the same happened with many activists in Egypt who began considering the Great October Revolution as a great revolutionary reference which has been helping them to understand the meaning of the revolutionary process and the nature of the revolutionary struggle against the counter revolution. Whatever the consequences were, the October Revolution was an illuminating sign in the memory of mankind when the collective will of the people touched the sky and turned into collective power which was capable of overthrowing tyranny and the repressive regime."

Binu Mathew, chief editor of the most influential left-wing electronic magazine in India, *Countercurrents.org* and my dear friend for many years, wrote from the city of Kochi, in Kerala State:

"The great October revolution made a huge impression among Indian revolutionaries and intellectuals in India. The Communist Party was formed on 26 December 1925 under the towering leadership of M. N. Roy. They organised against the British colonialists all over India. Major armed resistances took place in Telengana and Kerala. The communist party in Kerala formed a government in Kerala in 1957, the first time ever in the world a communist government was formed through the ballots. Communists now rule Kerala and Tripura. Their influence was lost in a major way in West Bengal due to its anti people policies. The communist party is not an influential player in India now. However they still have major influence in trade unions."

In the meantime, tens and some say hundreds of thousands of "Red Tourists" from China are descending on Russian cities, to commemorate the 100th anniversary of the October Revolution. Some will travel to St. Petersburg, others to Moscow or even Ulyanovsk, where V.I.

Lenin was born. Others will go as far as Georgia, to the birthplace of Stalin. China's President Xi Jinping encourages "Red Tourism". But most significantly, the great movement of people who are ready to commemorate most likely the greatest event of the 20th century is clearly proof and an indication that the world remembers, understands, and treasures the legacy of the monumental uprising, which shook the entire planet to its core.

Because of the determined propaganda and indoctrination, billions of people are confused. However, many are once again beginning to awaken and understand that it is not socialism that is outdated and obsolete. Outdated, inhuman, violent and deplorable are actually capitalism, colonialism and unrepentant Western imperialism, as well as their lackeys and prostitutes in media and education circles!

8

*I*n many great nations of the world, the principles and ideals of the October Revolution are alive and well. In places such as Russia itself, but also China, Vietnam, Cuba, Venezuela, Ecuador, Bolivia and lately even Syria and the Philippines, they form the core of the national identity as well as the mainstay of future development. There are dozens of other countries that were deeply influenced by this historic event.

But even in many countries that appear to be, at least on the surface, extremely far from being socialist, October Revolution's ideals, or at least some of them, have managed to domesticate - they gently penetrated the brains, hearts and souls of the people, and have stayed inside them, forever.

This is because they are correct, and because they reflect basic human dreams and aspirations.

Almost all human beings, no matter where they were born, what their race or culture is, are longing for solidarity, optimism, progress, safety, social justice, dignity and hope.

The Great October Socialist Revolution promised exactly those things, and more. Later, an enormous country and the system that were shaped on its ideals, managed to deliver a lot, although far from everything.

But 'everything' could and should never be 'delivered', by any system or a country. That is because any true Revolution is a tremendous journey; a process that never ends. It never is, or should be, the end.

First steps, first struggles, are always marked by courage, heroism, and sacrifices. That is where those who are weak, or not determined enough, often break; they betray and quickly return to their false, deceitful comfort zones.

Those who prevail and continue their struggle are then often burdened with even greater tasks: with the slow and tedious building of their country, with gradual step by step changes, with constant and overwhelming duties. They have to fight against all the negative inertia of so many, against reactionary forces and all sorts of disloyalties, against cowardice, and against fear.

There is always a great dose of cynicism slowing down the process, there is corruption especially at the lower levels, and there is constant interference, even interventions, from abroad. The enemy never sleeps, they say, and especially the enemy that has been hoping to control the entire world for eternity.

There are always plenty of 'objective reasons' why one should abandon the process, to give everything up, and to go back to bed, or back to familiar structures, be they the family, religion, 'culture' or class. Those who stumble, even those who betray out of fear, should be pitied, even helped back to their feet, but never judged too harshly. The enemies - reactionary forces and their preachers - are truly gruesome. For centuries they have been perfecting their 'art' of turning humans into scared, spineless, obedient, and submissive creatures.

True Revolution is like an icebreaker. The revolutionaries are its crew. The blizzard hits their faces, one false turn is made and everything is lost! An enormous vessel has to be steady; it has to be led decisively forward, with one single-minded goal: to bring the convoy of ships safely to calm and warm waters, to balminess and comfort, to a much better and kinder world. Thousands of lives of those in the vessels behind are in the hands of the captain of the icebreaker, and those at the control bridge, as well as the crew. It is so easy, when everything around is frozen and hostile and cold, to just give up, to lie down, to fall asleep, to freeze to death. It is so easy to jump into the cabin of the helicopter at the back of the ship, and escape, to fly away to safety and leave the rest to their terrible fate. But there are those human lives behind, thousands of them, and therefore, if one is on the control bridge, one fights and wins, for them, mainly for them, or he betrays, and goes down in history as a coward.

Or he fights like a hero, and still loses. In that case, others would soon rise, and finish what he began. That's how life is; that's how true revolutions are: the journey through the ice and blizzard, the journey that only the best of us would ever dare to embark on.

The Great October Socialist Revolution began by a proud salvo from *Aurora*. It broke the prison wall as well as chains, and a secret road suddenly opened. The journey began. Several countries rose, following the revolutionary ideals. Since then, some have fallen. Others have risen again.

The journey continues. It is the most beautiful, the most meaningful journey that I have ever took, and I have taken many. It is the toughest, the most demanding, and the most taxing journey. It is definitely not for the faint-hearted, it is not for the weak, not for those who have never grasped the true meaning of the word "Freedom".

But no matter what they say in London, Paris or New York, one thing is certain: even now, 'a Soviet man, it has a proud sound'!

Many have fallen. Many will fall. The enemy is fatal; it is mighty. But also love, humanism and the courage of our comrades are mighty. Mighty is the desire to build the most beautiful, optimistic, creative and kindest world imaginable!

*

Beirut – Kabul - Beirut
February-March 2017

About Author

Philosopher, novelist, filmmaker, investigative journalist, poet, playwright, and photographer, Andre Vltchek is a revolutionary, internationalist and globetrotter. In all his work, he confronts Western imperialism and the Western regime imposed on the world.

He has covered dozens of war zones and conflicts from Iraq and Peru to Sri Lanka, Bosnia, Rwanda, Syria, DR Congo and Timor-Leste.

His latest books are *Exposing Lies of the Empire*, *Fighting Against Western Imperialism* and *On Western Terrorism* with Noam Chomsky.

Aurora and *Point of No Return* are his major work of fiction, written in English. *Nalezeny* is his novel written in Czech. Other works include a book of political non-fiction, *Western Terror: From Potosi to Baghdad* and *Indonesia: Archipelago of*

Fear, also *Exile* (with Pramoedya Ananta Toer, and Rossie Indira) and *Oceania – Neocolonialism, Nukes & Bones.*

His plays are *'Ghosts of Valparaiso'* and *'Conversations with James'.*

He is a member of Advisory Committee of the BRussells Tribunal.

The investigative work of Andre Vltchek appears in countless publications worldwide.

Andre Vltchek has produced and directed several documentary films for the left-wing South American television network teleSUR. They deal with diverse topics, from Turkey/Syria to Okinawa, Kenya, Egypt and Indonesia, but all expose the effects of Western imperialism on the Planet. His feature documentary film *'Rwanda Gambit'* has been broadcasted by Press TV, and aims at reversing the official narrative on the 1994 genocide, as well as exposing the Rwandan and Ugandan plunder of DR Congo on behalf of Western imperialism. He produced the feature length documentary film about the Indonesian massacres of 1965 in *'Terlena – Breaking of The Nation*', as well as in his film about the brutal Somali refugee camp,

Dadaab, in Kenya: *'One Flew Over Dadaab'*. His Japanese crew filmed his lengthy discussion with Noam Chomsky on the state of the world, which is presently being made into a film.

He frequently speaks at revolutionary meetings, as well as at the principal universities worldwide.

He presently lives in Asia and the Middle East.

His website is http://andrevltchek.weebly.com/
And his Twitter is: @AndreVltchek

Compliments

This is a most excellent, important and timely essay!

~ George Burchett

EXPOSING LIES OF THE EMPIRE

Exposing Lies of The Empire is perhaps the most complete, and the most comprehensive account of the last several years, during which our planet has risen up and began its struggle against the Empire and its oppression. Vltchek takes us to all the continents, to slums and palaces, to the villages bombed into the ground, and to the front lines of the revolution. It alerts and provokes, clarifies and leads forward. It is a book of philosophy, a collection of exceptional investigative journalist reports,

and a manifesto. It will inspire millions. It will be quoted for centuries to come.

•••

"In an age of formula media, Andre Vltchek's work is truly exceptional -- fiercely independent and bracing in its challenges to the echoes and lies of the great power."
~ John Pilger

"Brave international correspondent and author Andre Vltchek has written countless essays and many books on the problems afflicting the world, from social injustice writ large, hidden institutionalized brutality, super- power hubris, and ecological murder, to the hypocrisy of entire cultures, beginning with the "Atlanticist civilization" that currently decimates the planet implementing the agendas of Washington's insatiable Neocons and a savage, cynical capitalism. Naturally, all of this is done in the name of those two sacred cows of all US world interventions: freedom and democracy...

This is one of Vltchek's most useful volumes, an anthology packed with the indispensable facts, first-hand knowledge, mature reflections, and righteous revolutionary furor necessary to combat the imperialist beast in all latitudes."

~ Patrice Greanville, *The Greanville Post*

"Exposing Lies of the Empire is a monumental work.

...the modus operandi of Andre Vltchek: go to the region, discover with purpose, and interview people from all walks of life to get the fullest possible local views, Weltanschauung, and insightful commentary on disparity along the power continuum.

... His reportages are about casting light on the ravages of western militarism and western rapacious capitalism for the rest of the world, pulling on the heart strings of the relatively comfortable people in the West...

In this book, readers can discover through Vltchek's words and photographs what life is like for the peoples embattled by insouciant capitalism in far-flung places: to name a few — Syria, Eritrea, China,

North Korea, Venezuela, Palestine, Viet Nam, and exotic locales few will have heard of, such as Kiribati.

Vltchek does not hold back as to what is harming people in the non-western lands. He points his finger — backed by evidence and compelling reasoning — at capitalists; capitalist's bloody henchmen, the military; empire's putschists and torturers; economic hitmen; collaborators; religious dogmatists; racists; the education (sic) system; media disinformation and propaganda; etc.

This is a book for everyone. Get it, read it, and become an informed citizen of earth. Find out what our broth- ers and sisters are resisting and solidarize with them. In particular, people who work within corporate journalism should read Exposing Lies of the Empire and find out what an authentic journalist really does."

~ Kim Petersen, *Dissident Voice*

POINT OF NO RETURN

Point of No Return shows the world through the eyes of a war correspondence, visiting places that are rarely covered by the mainstream media, offering provocative points of view about the pitiful state of today's world, its disparities and scandalous post-colonial arrangement – including global market fundamentalism and neo-conservative culture that are overthrowing democratic principals that humanity has fought for over centuries.

"André Vltchek is a writer, the real thing, of the same caliber and breed as Hemingway and Malraux."
~ Catherine Merveilleux

"Andre Vltchek tells us about a world that few know, even when they think they do. That is because he tells the truth, vividly, with a keen sense of history, and with a perceptive eye that sees past surfaces to reality..."
~ Noam Chomsky

"Point of No Return is one of the great novels of the 21st century. It deserves a wide readership and serious critical appraisal. Over a half century ago, in his important book "American Moderns - From Rebellion to Conformity," the great literary critic Maxwell Geismar noted "Our best literary work has come from writers who are outside [the dominant] intellectual orbit, where [capitalist] panic has slowly subsided into inertia." Geismar anticipates Vltchek. Point of No Return explodes from that vital realm far beyond hegemonic control."
~ Tony Christini, author of *Homefront*

"Point of No Return is riveting."
> ~ Paulin Cesari, *Le Figaro*

"A fascinating look at the world through the eyes of a war correspondent – a world few of us know."
> ~ Eve Jackson, *France24*

"Once again, it's the context that makes the book. It is quite simply mind-boggling. Andre Vltchek knows very well what he's talking about (...). It is a book that cannot fail to move, a rich, strong and dense tale, by all means get a hold of a copy for an intelligent read!"
> ~ Yves Mabon

"Quite simply a masterpiece... All of the absurdity of our society, its lack of humanity and sense blows up in our face... All readers will feel touched by this narrative that speaks of liberty, choice and our place in the world."
> ~ Stephanie Morelli

"A splendid novel that will leave no one cold. The author skilfully takes us along on

a mysterious and sorrowful journey. A gripping read."
~ Patrick Martinez - *Radio Coteaux*

"André Vltchek offers an unsparing portrait of the world we live in. With his provocative outlook, he lays bare a situation that is really quite simple, and did not begin yesterday... Although this book does not raise easy questions, it is indeed easy to read, thanks to the wit and subtlety of its author."
~ Françoise Bachelet

"Andre Vltchek's work has the incredible capacity of helping one break free from the culture of denial. His ability to translate reality into fiction is stunningly original and very personal. His work shocks you while at the same time reconnect you with the political realities of today. Wisdom can only from a clear understanding of the past and some brutal honesty. This is the purpose of Andre's political novels."
~ Anuradha Mittal, *The Oakland Institute*

"... despite all the terror and despite somber analyses about the battle between "market fundamentalists and religious fundamentalists" being the main contradiction of our time, Vltchek's novel projects the same desperate hope that once emanated from *Man's Fate* by André Malraux or *To Whom the Bells Toll* by Ernest Hemingway ... And as a matter of fact, Vltchek evokes strong memories of them, but not just because of his reawakening of the buried tradition of political fiction, but also because of his immense narrative talent ... Just like authors as Dan Chodorokoff, Ron Jacob, and others, Andre Vltchek is turning another chapter in the history of American literature."

~ Michael Schiffmann

Printed in Great Britain
by Amazon